What Do I Eat?

by

SHIRLEY GREENWAY

photographs by

OXFORD SCIENTIFIC FILMS

Ideals Children's Books   Nashville, Tennessee

Published by Ideals Publishing Corporation
Nashville, Tennessee 37214

Printed and bound in the United States of America.

Created and designed by Treld Bicknell.

Library of Congress Cataloging-in-Publication Data

Greenway, Shirley.
What do I eat?/by Shirley Greenway; photographs
by Oxford Scientific Films.
p. cm.
Includes index.
Summary: Explains the diet and feeding habits of such
animals as the hippopotamus, leopard slug, and pelica
ISBN 0-8249-8627-X (lib. bdg.)
ISBN 0-8249-8602-4 (trade pbk.)
1. Animals — Food — Miscellanea —Juvenile literatur
[1. Animals — Food habits.] I. Oxford Scientific Films
II. Title. III. Series. Greenway, Shirley, Animals Q & A
QL756.5.G74   1993
591.53—dc20   93-185
                                                       CIP
                                                       AC

Acknowledgments:
The author and publisher wish to thank the following for permission to reproduce copyright material: **Oxford
Scientific Films** for front cover and p. 19 (Michael Fogden); title page and p. 27 (Animals Animals [AA]—Kojo
Tanaka); p. 3 (Mantis Wildlife Films—Densey Clyne); p. 4 (Partridge Films Ltd.—Richard Foster); p. 5 (AA—Breck
Kent); pp. 6-7 (Peter Parks); p. 8 (AA—E.R. Degginger); p. 9 (Mark Hamblin); p. 10 (AA—Zig Leszczynski); pp. 10-
(Howard Hall); p. 13 (AA—Zig Leszczynski); pp. 12-13 (Frank Schneidermeyer); p. 14 (Press-Tige Pictures); p. 15
(Barrie E. Watts); pp. 16, 24, 25, and **29 (G.I. Bernard)**; p. 17 (Kathie Atkinson); p. 18 (David Curl); p. 20 (Stan
Osolinski); pp. 22-23 (P. & W. Ward); **p. 26 (AA**—Fran Allan); p. 28 (Max Gibbs); back cover (David Thompson).

Q. I am a honeybee. What do I eat?

A. Honeybee workers feed from bright flowers, taking sweet nectar and yellow pollen, which they store in their leg "baskets." They don't eat it all—they carry much of it back to the hive where it is kept as honey for the baby bees, or grubs.

Q. I am an anteater. How do I catch my food?

A. The soft-furred Tamandua anteater lives in the trees of South American forests. It hunts for the nests of ants and termites, holding onto branches with its long, sensitive tail. Using curved, sharp claws, the anteater can break open the hard clay shell of an ants' nest. Then it pokes its long snout into the broken nest and scoops up ants with its thin, sticky tongue.

Q. I am a sea jelly.
What do I eat?

A. The Portuguese man-o'-war bobs along with its gas-filled float above the water — like the sail of a ship. Under the water, its long, curly, stinging tentacles act as waving fishing lines. With these, the sea jelly catches, stings, and reels in small fish.

Q. I am a hippopotamus. What do I eat?

A. The huge, smooth-skinned hippopotamus spends the hot African days resting up to its nose in cool water. When evening comes, it trundles along a well-worn path to a favorite grazing spot and spends the night hours eating grass.

Q. I am an iguana.
What do I eat?

A. The green iguana is a large, handsome Central and South American lizard with a spiked crest and a thick, heavy tail. Its pale green scales make it almost invisible as it moves among the rainforest trees. The huge iguana looks fierce but it isn't dangerous to smaller creatures. It feeds only on fruit and flower petals!

▷

Q. I am a vole.
What do I eat?

A. The tiny mouse-like bank vole lives
well hidden in a woody bramble
thicket. Sitting very still it listens for
danger signs, then scurries forward to
seize a dropped seed or a plump
blackberry. Holding its food with
delicate, long-fingered paws, the vole
quickly nibbles its juicy meal.
Voles love to eat—up to one-and-a-
half times their own weight each day.

Q. I am a slug.
What do I eat?

A. Slugs can be striped or spotted, and colored in orange, yellow, and shiny black. These large, three- to eight-inch long, shell-less snails creep along the ground or along tree branches eating roots and dead leaves. But the huge spotted leopard slug feeds only on fungi, such as mushrooms and toadstools.

Q. I am a snake.
What do I eat?

A. The African egg-eater snake lives entirely on birds' eggs, which it can locate by smell. The snake coils itself around the egg and unhinges its jaws to swallow it whole. As the snake moves, rough bones in its throat saw through the hard shell. When it has swallowed the contents of the egg, the snake spits out the crushed shell.

Q. I am a pelican.

How do I catch my food?

A. The brown pelican is a tall and impressive bird that loves fishing. Flying low over the water, the pelican can spot a shoal of fish glittering as they leap among the waves. With a darting dive, the pelican emerges with its huge, pouched beak filled with fish.

▶

Q. I am a sea anemone.
What do I eat?

A. The beautiful, flower-like sea anemone (uh-NEM-uh-nee) is actually a hungry animal predator. Its brightly colored tentacles are covered with stinging cells. They wave gently in the water to trap small shrimp and tiny fish, which they bring to the anemone's ever-open mouth.

Q. I am a giant panda.
What do I eat?

A. Giant pandas eat only bamboo stems and leaves, which they grip with a unique bony "thumb" on each hand. The slow, heavy panda sits and pulls the tall, swaying stems down until they break. But bamboo isn't very nourishing and pandas may eat up to 500 stems each day.

Q. I am a fish.

How do I catch my food?

A. Like many fish that come up to the surface to hunt, the archerfish likes to catch an unwary insect. This aptly named black and gold fish fills its mouth with water and makes a tube with its tongue and upper jaw. Then it "shoots" down its prey with a well-aimed spurt of water—from as far as six feet away!

The honeybee
eats nectar
and pollen.

The hipp
grazes
on grass.

The anteater
feeds on ants
and termites.

The igua
eats fruit
and flowe

The sea jelly
eats small
fish.

The vole
eats seeds
and berri

 The slug eats fungi.

 The sea anemone eats shrimps.

 The egg-eater snake swallows eggs.

 The giant panda feeds on bamboo.

 The pelican eats fish.

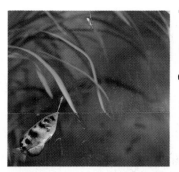 The archerfish eats insects.

31

Index